How Do They Grow?

From Chick to Chicken

by Jillian Powell

Hodder
Wayland

an imprint of Hodder Children's Books

© 2001 White-Thomson Publishing Ltd

Produced for Hodder Wayland by
White-Thomson Publishing Ltd
2/3 St. Andrew's Place
Lewes, East Sussex
BN7 1UP

Editor: Sarah Doughty
Designer: Tessa Barwick
Text consultant: Jessica Buss
Language consultant: Norah Granger

Published in Great Britain in 2001 by Hodder Wayland,
an imprint of Hodder Children's Books.

British Library Cataloguing in Publication Data
    Powell, Jillian
        From chick to chicken. – (How do they grow?)
        1. Chickens – Development – Juvenile literature 2. Chickens –
        Physiology – Juvenile literature
        I. Title
        636.5

ISBN 0 7502 3868 2

Printed and bound in Italy by G. Canale & C.S.p.A.

Hodder Children's Books
A division of Hodder Headline Ltd
338 Euston Road, London NW1 3BH

Contents

Words in **bold** in the text can be found in the glossary on page 30.

From egg to chick

4

This **hen** has laid some eggs.
She has made a nest of straw.
She sits on the eggs to keep them
safe and warm until they **hatch**.

On this farm, the hens are kept with **cockerels**. When the hens **mate** with the cockerels, baby chicks can grow inside the eggs that the hens lay.

Inside the eggs

A hen lays an egg almost every day.
Each egg rolls into her nest. The eggshells are
strong so the chicks can grow safely inside them.

6

Inside each egg is a pocket of air so the chick can breathe. The yellow **yolk** is food for the baby bird as it grows.

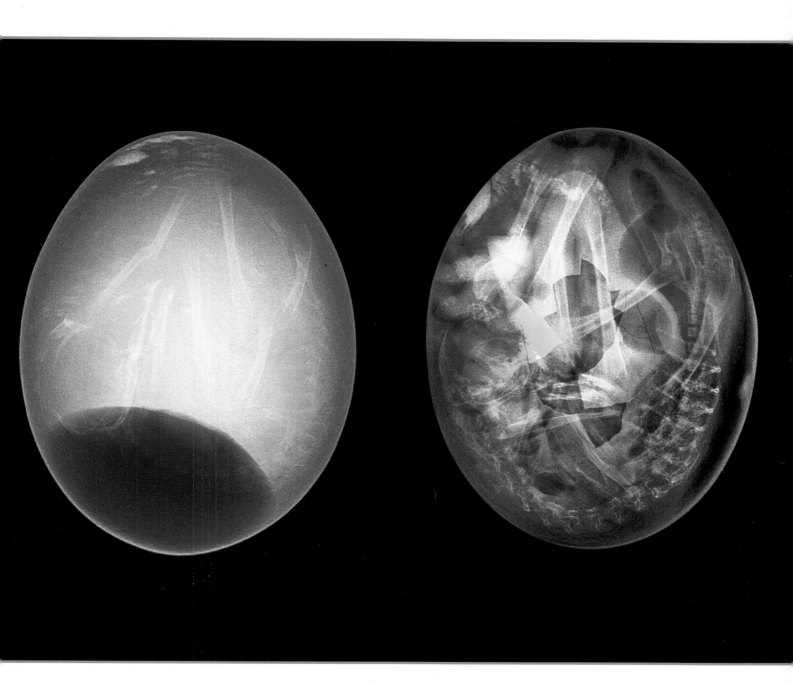

Ready to hatch

After 21 days the baby chick is ready to hatch. It breaks its way out of the shell using a sharp point on its beak. This is called its egg tooth.

This chick has just hatched. Its wings are tiny and its feet are big for its body. Its coat is wet at first. It soon becomes dry and fluffy.

Young chicks

The chicks stay close to their mother.
She keeps them safe and warm. They will
follow her everywhere.

These chicks are just a day old. Their coats are yellow and fluffy. When they are older, they will grow feathers like their mother's.

At the hatchery

On big farms, chicks hatch out from eggs in a **hatchery**. The eggs are kept in trays which keep them safe and warm, just like a mother hen does.

The eggs are turned several times a day, just like a hen turns the eggs in her nest. Twenty-one days after the eggs have been laid they hatch into chicks.

Hatchery chicks

In a hatchery, lots of chicks hatch out together. These chicks often go to **broiler farms**. On a broiler farm chicks will grow until they are big enough to give us chicken meat.

Females can be chosen from a batch of chicks. These females go to egg farms where hens lay eggs for people to eat.

At the broiler farm

A farm worker is placing these chicks in the broiler shed. They will spend their lives in this shed, where they will grow quickly.

These chicks are now seven days old. They have plenty of food and water to drink. The chicks are feeding on food made from **grains** which helps them to grow.

Chickens for meat

These chicks are a few weeks old. As they get bigger, feathers replace their soft yellow coats. When they are five to eight weeks old, they will be big enough to sell for meat.

These broiler chickens are kept on a **free-range farm**. This means they spend part of their lives outdoors and can scratch around outside to find food. The chickens are now fully grown.

The egg farm

On an egg farm, the farmer keeps female chicks. These chicks will grow into hens that lay eggs for people to eat. The lamp is keeping the chicks warm.

These young hens are six weeks old. They hatched in the spring. They will be ready to start laying their own eggs in the autumn.

Free-range hens

This hen is 20 weeks old. Her wings and feathers are now fully grown. She is ready to lay her own eggs. These eggs will be sold for people to eat.

Hens kept on free-range egg farms can go outdoors in the daytime. They sleep in the hen house at night to keep them safe from foxes.

23

Laying eggs to eat

Hens kept on free-range farms lay their eggs in nesting boxes like this. The box is in a hen house. This means the hen and her eggs are safe and warm in the straw nest.

24

This farm worker is collecting free-range eggs.
The eggs roll out of the nesting boxes.
The farm worker puts them into trays.

The breeding farm

Some female chicks grow into hens that are kept for **breeding**. They live in breeding sheds and are given plenty of grain to help them lay lots of eggs.

26

The farmer keeps cockerels to mate with the hens. When they have mated, baby chicks start to grow inside the eggs that the hens lay.

Eggs for hatching

After the hens have laid their eggs they are collected from the nest boxes at the breeding house. The best eggs go to the hatchery and are kept warm in trays.

This chick has just hatched from an egg at the hatchery. Hens can lay eggs every day so chicks are hatched all through the year.

Glossary

Breeding When a male and female produce young.

Broiler farm A farm which produces chickens for meat. They are called broilers.

Cockerels Male chickens.

Free-range farm A farm that allows its chickens or hens to go outdoors in the daytime.

Grains The seeds of cereal crops like wheat and maize.

Hatch When a baby bird breaks out of its eggshell.

Hatchery A place where eggs are kept warm in trays before the chicks hatch.

Hen A female chicken.

Mate When a male and female come together to have babies. A male gives a female a seed which makes a baby bird grow inside her eggs.

Yolk The yellow part of the inside of an egg. It is food for a growing chick.

Further information

Books

A First Look at Animals on the Farm by James, Lynn and Dodds (Two Can Publishing, 2000)

Animals on the Farm by Sally Morgan (Franklin Watts, 1999)

Chick (See How they Grow series, Dorling Kindersley, 1993)

Chickens (Farm Animals series) by Rachael Bell (Heinemann, 2000)

From Egg to Chicken (Life Cycles series) by David Salariya (Franklin Watts, 1997)

Life Cycle of a Chicken by Angela Royston (Heinemann, 1998)

Poultry Farm (Let's Visit a Farm series) by Sarah Doughty and Diana Bentley (Hodder Wayland, 1989)

Video

On the Farm: Baby Animals (Dorling Kindersley)

The Chicken and the Egg (National Farmer's Union)

Websites

www.britegg.co.uk
The website of the British Egg Information Service, which provides lots of facts about eggs and egg production. It includes 'egg fun' with a competition.

www.aeb.org
The American egg board site has all sorts of information about eggs and poultry, with egg facts and an 'eggcyclopaedia'.

Useful addresses

The National Association of Farms for Schools provides an annual directory of farms providing facilities for school visits, and an information line. To find out more, write to 164, Shaftesbury Avenue, London WC2H 8HL (tel: 01422 882 708) or visit their website at: **www.farmsforschools.org.uk**

The Food and Farming Education Service provides a directory of learning resources for primary and secondary schools and a list of local resource centres. To find out more write to Stoneleigh Park, Warwickshire, CV8 2LZ (tel: 02476 535 707) or visit their website at: **www.foodandfarming.org**

Index

B

beak 8

breathing 7

breeding sheds 26

broiler farm 14, 16

C

chicks 5, 6, 7, 8, 9,
10, 11, 12, 13, 14,
15, 16, 17, 18, 20,
26, 27, 29

cockerels 5, 27

E

egg farms 15, 20-21,

egg tooth 8

eggs 4, 5, 6, 7, 12, 13,
15, 20, 21, 22, 24,
25, 26, 27, 28, 29

F

feathers 11, 18, 22

food 7, 17, 19

foxes 23

free-range farms 19,
22-5

H

hatchery 12, 14, 28,
29

hatching 4, 8, 9, 12,
13, 14, 29

M

mating 5, 27

meat 14, 18

N

nest 4, 6, 13, 24

nesting boxes 24, 25

W

water 17

wings 9, 22

Y

yolk 7

Picture acknowledgements

Agripicture (Peter Dean) 12, 13, 14, 15, 28, 29; FLPA 4 (W. Adams/Sunset),
10 (Derek Middleton), 20 (John Watkins), 21 (John Watkins), 26 (Gerard Laci);
Holt Studios International 16 (Inga Spence) 17 (Nigel Cattlin); 24 (Inga Spence);
HWPL 18, 25; NHPA 6 (David Woodfall), 8 (E. A Janes), 9 (E. A Janes); RSPCA
Photolibrary title page (Jeff du Fea), 5 (E. A Janes), 11 (E. A Janes), 19 (Colin
Seddon), 22 (Angela Hampton), 23 (Andrew Linscott), 27 (E. A Janes); Science Photo
Library 7 (Hugh Turvey).